Winter is the coldest time of the year.
You need to wear warm clothes outside.

Now try this
Does the picture opposite show a winter scene?
How can you tell?

3

Very, very slowly, near the end of winter, things begin to change.
The weather begins to become warmer.
Snow or ice left over from the winter starts to melt.
Each day, darkness comes a little bit later.

Try this later
Put an ice cube on a saucer on a sunny windowsill.
What happens to it?

4

In spring, grey and white clouds
sometimes cover the sky.
Rain begins to fall.

Then the breeze blows the clouds away and the sun shines again.

Lots of daylight, sunshine and rain are what plants need to begin to grow again.

Fat buds appear on the bare trees. Soon they will open out into leaves and flowers.

9

Gardeners know that it is time to plant seeds to grow new plants. They dig the ground and carefully put the tiny seeds in the soil.

Try this later

Fill the holes in a cardboard egg box with soil.
Plant a seed in each hole.
Put the egg box on a sunny windowsill and
water it a little every day.
Wait to see what happens!

Under the earth, some plants have already been busy growing.

Soon lots of spring bulbs push up shoots.
The shoots become leaves and flower buds.

Before long, the bulbs are in full flower.

As the plants begin to grow and
the weather becomes warmer,
birds can find more to eat.
It is time to build their nests and
lay their eggs.

Try this later
Look out for broken egg shells
under trees and hedges.
Ask someone to help you find out
what kind of birds laid them.

Spring is also the time when
lots of other animals have babies.

Now try this
Baby sheep are called lambs.
How many other special names for baby animals
can you think of?

In ponds and lakes, frogs lay
eggs called frogspawn.
They hatch into little tadpoles.
Slowly the tadpoles grow into
small frogs.

In spring, people all over the world hold special festivals to celebrate this time of new beginnings.

How do you celebrate the spring?

In springtime, everything is
growing and changing.
The weather slowly becomes
warmer and warmer until...
it's not spring any more but summer!

Try this later

Find out if someone in your family or a friend has a birthday in the spring. Make them a card showing all the things about spring that you like best.

Index

© 1996 Watts Books

Watts Books
96 Leonard Street
London
EC2A 4RH

Franklin Watts Australia
14 Mars Road
Lane Cove
NSW 2066

ISBN: 0 7496 2337 3

Dewey Decimal Classification
Number 574.5

A CIP catalogue record for this
book is available from the British
Library.

Editor: Sarah Ridley
Designer: Kirstie Billingham
Picture researcher: Sarah Moule

Acknowledgements: the publishers
would like to thank Carol Olivier and
Kenmont Primary School for their help
with the cover for this book.

Photographs: Clic/Clac Impact Photos
20; Bruce Coleman Ltd 9, 13, 19; Eye
Ubiquitous 5; Chris Fairclough Colour
Library 22; Robert Harding Photo
Library 17; NHPA 3, 10; Peter Millard
front cover; ZEFA 15.

Printed in Malaysia